AMERICA

whitecap

Photo selection, photo editing, cover layout, and interior design by Jan Westendorp
Text by Sarah Maitland

Copyright of the photographs is retained by the photographer. See page 112 for photo credits.

Printed in China

Library and Archives Canada Cataloguing in Publication

Maitland, Sarah, 1984–
        America / [text by Sarah Maitland ; photo selection, editing and interior design by Jan Westendorp].

(America series)
ISBN 978-1-77050-010-5

        1. United States—Pictorial works. I. Westendorp, Jan II. Title. III. Series: America series

E169.Z83A45 2010   973.93022'2   C2010-900913-4

The publisher acknowledges the financial support of the Government of Canada through the Canada Book Fund (CBF) and the Province of British Columbia through the Book Publishing Tax Credit.

For more information on the America series and other titles from Whitecap Books, please visit our website at www.whitecap.ca.

The United States of America is a land of constant movement and exploration. From the seasonal migration of ancient Native Americans and the westward drives of early European explorers to the upward push of towering skyscrapers and grand monuments, there's always something on the go in America.

Even America's physical geography is the result of dynamic forces. Thousands of years ago glaciers inched across what is now America, carving the jagged peaks and deep lakes of the Rocky Mountains, and forming rolling fields and prairie potholes. The Colorado River gradually eroded the Grand Canyon, and the recession of an inland sea exposed the looming Chalk Pyramids of Kansas. And America's natural landscape is still evolving—the Kilauea volcano on the big island of Hawaii emits enough lava in one day to cover a two-lane road for 20 miles.

Ancient indigenous peoples constantly traveled across America, following herds and searching for perfect locations to cultivate land. In the course of their travels they left amazing artifacts scattered across America, like the abandoned cliffside structures in the Canyon de Chelly, on Navajo Nation land.

Europeans began moving into America in the 14th and 15th centuries, with settlements forming along the East Coast from the Florida Keys to Boston. Pioneers and explorers then paved the way to the West, like Meriwether Lewis and William Clark, who left Illinois in 1804 to discover an overland route to the Pacific Ocean, record the mysterious geography and biology of the West, and search for potential places to settle. Rustic hamlets quickly developed, leading to the modern marvels of today's cities, which include soaring skyscrapers in New York City and architectural works of art, like the Rock and Roll Hall of Fame in Cleveland.

It would take a lifetime to explore all that America has to offer: from the human-made monuments of the Statue of Liberty and Golden Gate Bridge to the natural wonders of the Grand Canyon and Old Faithful geyser. America's 50 states encompass almost 3,800,000 square miles, contain 392 spectacular national parks, and boast 9 bustling cities each with more than a million inhabitants. Every turn of the page invites you to take another step into the vast visual landscape of America.

OVERLEAF—
The sun rises over calm coastal waters in Acadia National Park, Maine. The park is famous for a natural phenomenon called Thunder Hole, a small rocky inlet that reverberates with a thunderous crack when waves crash into it.

RIGHT—
The Glade Creek Grist Mill in Babcock State Park, West Virginia, was constructed in 1975 using pieces of three old mills in the area. It stands as a working monument to the mills of the past, and produces ground cornmeal and buckwheat flour with the help of a stream.

Vermont has more covered bridges per square mile than anywhere else in the world. The bridges were originally covered to protect the wood from rotting and to keep carriage horses from slipping on wet boards. Their shadowy recesses earned them the nickname "kissing bridges."

A country road winds past Gypsy Woods Farm in Connecticut. Farmland covers only a small percentage of the state, but family-owned farms provide a lovely contrast to the state's urban centers of New Haven and Hartford.

New York's Central Park is the best known and most visited urban park in the United States. The park was established on more than 800 acres of land during the mid-19th century, and provides locals and tourists with a welcome respite in the middle of the Manhattan bustle.

More than 25 million European immigrants were processed at the Ellis Island immigration station in Manhattan between 1892 and 1924. The ancestors of more than 40 percent of America's current population entered the country via this New York port, which is now a museum.

The Statue of Liberty stands watch over Upper New York Bay. The monument was a gift to the Americans from the French in 1886, and has since become a symbol of freedom and democracy. In 1986 the original torch was replaced with a copper torch covered in 24-karat gold leaf.

Mercury, the god of speed, perches atop Grand Central Station and reaches toward the Chrysler Building (right). The Chrysler Building was completed in 1930 during New York's skyscraper boom, and the builder and architect kept the dazzling spire's design a secret until it was erected.

Lights on the Brooklyn Bridge, and the Manhattan and Williamsburg bridges behind it, are reflected in the East River. In 1884, showman P. T. Barnum squelched fears that the Brooklyn Bridge was unstable when his elephant Jumbo led a parade of 21 elephants across it.

The Egg performing arts center in Albany, New York's state capital, houses two theaters with a combined seating capacity of more than 1,400. The Egg sits in the Governor Nelson A. Rockefeller Empire State Plaza, and was designed by Wallace Harrison, the architect who also created the United Nations headquarters.

The grand arch of the Boston Harbor Hotel spans a spacious public plaza that guides pedestrians from downtown Boston, Massachusetts, to Rowes Wharf. The marina houses luxury yachts, commuter boats, and a floating dock where free summer concerts are held.

17

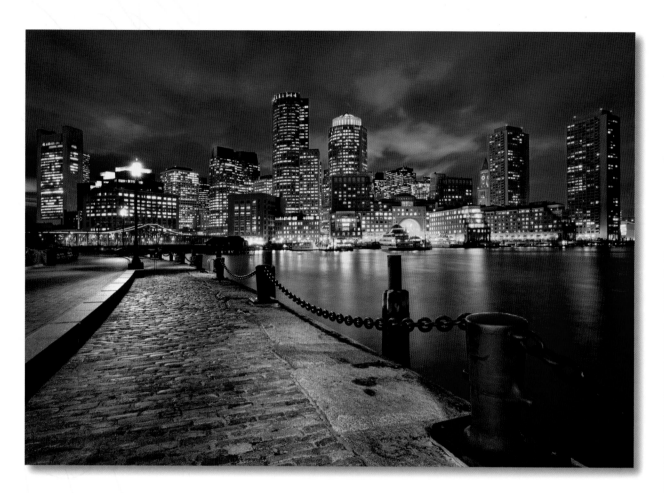

Boston Harbor, with its skyscrapers aglow at dusk, has changed substantially since the time of the Boston Tea Party, but some of its cobblestones from ages past still endure.

Over the centuries, many people have walked Boston's Long Wharf, from shackled pirates to royal governors. The Gardiner Building (right foreground) dates from the 1760s, and is the oldest surviving structure on the wharf.

Salem, Massachusetts, was once an important seaport. During the American Revolution, ships from Salem captured hundreds of British vessels in a process called privateering, where civilian captains captured enemy ships, sailed them back to America, and then sold the cargo.

Pleasure boats now moor in the harbor of Nantucket Island, Massachusetts, which was considered the whaling capital of the world until 1838, when petroleum replaced whale oil as a light source. Herman Melville's novel *Moby-Dick* was inspired by the *Essex,* the Nantucket whaleship that was attacked by a whale and sank in 1820.

The Edgartown Harbor Light is one of five lighthouses on Martha's Vineyard, a grapevine-covered island seven miles from the Massachusetts mainland. The English explorer Bartholomew Gosnold named the island after either his daughter or his mother-in-law, who apparently financed his expedition.

Gettysburg National Military Park in Pennsylvania preserves the site of the bloodiest Civil War battle, with 51,000 casualties. Like the George Weikert House in the background, all of the churches, public buildings, and houses in the area became temporary hospitals after the battle, and the farmers' fields became graveyards.

During the American Revolution, George Washington, his wife, and his staff all spent the winter of 1777–78 in this house at the Valley Forge encampment in Pennsylvania. The harsh conditions at the encampment led to more than 2,000 soldier deaths from disease.

Independence National Historical Park in Philadelphia, Pennsylvania, contains both Independence Hall, where the Declaration of Independence and the United States Constitution were signed, and the cracked Liberty Bell, which used to ring from the hall's tower.

Pennsylvania, named after the Quaker William Penn, is home to the Pennsylvania Dutch—members of the Amish, Mennonite, and Brethren sects—who have farmed in Lancaster County for centuries. They use horses both to work their farms and to pull buggies, which are used for transportation.

Evening light sets grasses ablaze at Timber Hollow Overlook in Shenandoah National Park, Virginia. Native Americans have enjoyed the beauty of the Shenandoah Mountains for more than 8,000 years. Many of their tools were made from stones found in the area.

The US federal government meets in the Capitol building in Washington, DC. The dome that sits atop the building has been reconstructed twice: after British troops set fire to the building during the War of 1812, and after building expansions dwarfed the previous dome.

For more than 200 years, the White House has been the official residence and workplace of the president of the United States. The building sits on 18 acres of manicured gardens in Washington, DC.

Ocracoke Island is one of the many Outer Banks barrier islands that separate North Carolina's mainland from the Atlantic Ocean. These islands served as shelter for many pirates, and the infamous Blackbeard fought and lost his final duel in the waters near Ocracoke.

The Cape Hatteras Lighthouse, the tallest brick lighthouse in North America, warns ships of the "Graveyard of the Atlantic" off the shore of North Carolina. Its black and white stripes make it visible during the day, and its unique light sequence at night distinguishes it from other lighthouses.

The 1,700 islands that make up the Florida Keys got their name from explorers who called them *cayos*, Spanish for "islands." Just over 40 bridges connect more than 100 of the islands.

The pinelands of Florida's Everglades National Park need fire to thrive, so the park staff carry out controlled burns that mimic natural fires. Burns eliminate light-blocking plants so the sun can reach slash pine seedlings, and the saw palmettos beneath the trees resprout and return to their preburn condition within a year.

Brightly colored geometric designs were used to cover the outside of Mission Concepción in Texas, but they faded long ago. However, since the original 1755 roof still protects the interior, sections of painstakingly painted frescoes still line the inside walls.

Five thousand species of flowering plants, like these Indian paintbrushes and bluebonnets, bloom in the grasslands that cover much of Texas.

The banks of the San Antonio River in Texas are lined with pedestrian walkways, restaurants, and shops.
In January the river is drained for maintenance, and its refilling begins the Mud Festival, which includes
a floating parade and the crowning of a mud king and queen.

Rice farming began in Fort Bend County, Texas, in the late 1800s. Farmers work extremely hard during rice-growing season to ensure fresh water is always flowing over the crop. When the fields turn yellow, they are drained and harvested.

The Misión San Antonio de Valero, founded by Spanish missionaries in 1718, was the site of the 1836 Battle of the Alamo, in which fewer than 200 Texans defended the by-then renamed Alamo Mission to the death against a Mexican force of more than 5,000.

The Chisos Mountains in Big Bend National Park, Texas, glow red behind the cool blue-green succulent leaves of century plants. These plants, which are a type of agave, grow for 20 to 50 years before blooming just once and then dying.

Water trickles through a natural bridge carved out of rock and tumbles into the Buffalo National River in Arkansas. The river is a popular camping and recreation area, and hikers can explore more than 100 miles of maintained trails throughout the park.

The Gateway Arch in St. Louis, Missouri, forms an oval with its reflection in the Mississippi River. It is the highest monument in the country at 630 feet (192 meters), and visitors can take a tram to the observation deck at the top of the arch.

Missouri is a major agricultural producer; livestock outnumber humans by over a million head. Missouri is also the home state of well-known authors Mark Twain, T. S. Eliot, and Maya Angelou.

Young corn absorbs the last evening light in LaSalle County, Illinois. Farmland covers the majority of Illinois, and corn and soybeans are the main crops grown here.

The south tower of the classically inspired Wrigley Building on Chicago's Magnificent Mile boasts a four-sided clock. The Tribune Tower, on the right, has rocks from landmarks in all 50 states and from international sites like the Parthenon and the Taj Mahal embedded in its base.

Chicago's Lincoln Park lies along the western shore of Lake Michigan. Once the site of several cemeteries, the area has now been repurposed into a large park that includes a conservatory, a museum, and an outdoor theater.

The window-lined entrance hall of the Quadracci Pavilion at the Milwaukee Art Museum in Milwaukee, Wisconsin, extends over Lake Michigan like the prow of a ship. Designed by Santiago Calatrava and completed in 2001, the pavilion contains an auditorium, exhibition space, a café, and parking.

The first rock-and-roll concert took place in Cleveland, Ohio, in 1952, and the city is now home to the Rock and Roll Hall of Fame and Museum. Architect I. M. Pei's design of the Hall of Fame entrance echoes his controversial glass pyramid at the Louvre.

Farmland covers the majority of Iowa, but less than 6 percent of Iowa's population lives on that land. In 1804 explorers Lewis and Clark traveled 300 miles up the Missouri River, which runs along the Iowa-Nebraska border, as a part of their overland expedition from the east to the West Coast.

Iowa produces millions of bushels of soybeans a year. Some of the beans are fed to farm animals, but others are used to make a variety of products, from crayons to soy biodiesel.

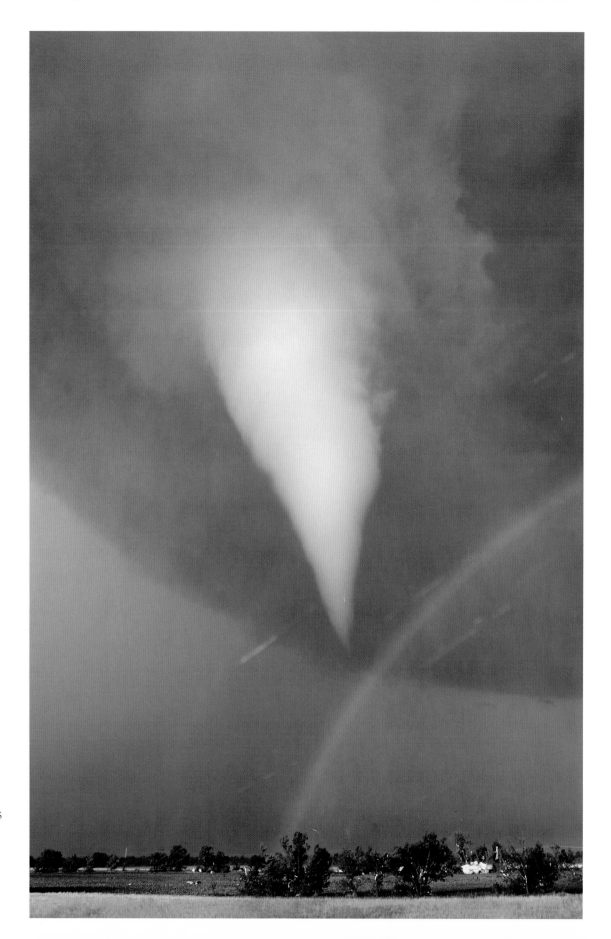

A rainbow forms while the funnel of a tornado recedes, and hailstones rain down on rural Kansas. Located in Tornado Alley, the state of Kansas is hit by an average of 50 tornadoes a year.

The Monument Rocks, or Chalk Pyramids, of Kansas are sedimentary formations that were created 80 million years ago when the Great Plains were an inland sea. The rocks contain ancient sea fossils, and the highest stand over 70 feet (21 meters) high.

Ancient glaciers created the prairie potholes of North Dakota, which now fill with spring rain and snowmelt, and provide a home for marsh birds. Farmers often drain the potholes, and only half of the region's original wetlands remain.

It took hundreds of workers, under the direction of sculptor Gutzon Borglum, to immortalize presidents George Washington, Thomas Jefferson, Theodore Roosevelt, and Abraham Lincoln in the granite of South Dakota's Mount Rushmore. The project began in 1927 and was completed in 1941.

Gradual erosion exposed Devils Tower, which overlooks the Belle Fourche River in Wyoming. In 1906, President Theodore Roosevelt named Devils Tower America's first National Monument.

Glaciers carved the rugged peaks and crystal lakes of Glacier National Park in northern Montana. The park encompasses more than a million acres and is home to threatened and endangered species like lynx, grizzly bears, and gray wolves.

Yellowstone National Park, which spans Wyoming, Montana, and Idaho, was the first national park in the world. There are more than 300 geysers within the preserve. Old Faithful in Wyoming is the most famous, spraying hot water and steam every 35 to 120 minutes.

Fifty miles of the Snake River wind through Wyoming's Grand Teton National Park. The summit of the Grand Teton rises more than 7,000 feet (2,134 meters) above the valley floor of Jackson Hole.

For centuries, the Pueblo people of Santa Fe, New Mexico, have constructed adobe structures from sun-dried bricks made of clay, sand, and silt. Today, the city's zoning code states that even new buildings must adhere to the old Spanish-Pueblo look of adobe buildings.

New Mexico's White Sands National Monument was once a prehistoric sea, which retreated and left behind gypsum crystals that the wind churned and molded into immense dunes. Outside the park, the first atomic bomb was tested at the White Sands Missile Range.

While plant and animal life flourishes on the Grand Canyon's rim, the inner canyon is mainly desert, with temperatures soaring much higher than those above. The average depth of the canyon is 4,000 feet (1,219 meters), and the deepest point is 6,000 feet (1,829 meters).

It is fitting that the East and West Mitten Buttes resemble warm winter mittens—because of Monument Valley Navajo Tribal Park's high elevation, the average temperature in Monument Valley, Arizona, drops to 25 degrees Fahrenheit (−4 degrees Celsius) in winter. The park is on the Navajo Indian Reserve, which protects Navajo ancestral territory and traditional ways of life.

Just outside Page, Arizona, the Colorado River cuts a dramatic path through Glen Canyon at Horseshoe Bend. The Colorado flows through seven American states and two Mexican states before emptying into the Gulf of California.

FACING PAGE—

Organ Pipe Cactus National Monument in Arizona protects hundreds of thousands of acres of green desert and contains many different species of cacti, including the tall saguaro. The park's namesake cactus can live up to 150 years, and it takes 35 years to produce its first flower.

RIGHT—

Shafts of sunlight shine down Arizona's Antelope Canyon, located on the land of the LeChee Chapter of the Navajo Nation. Most of the time, the canyon is dry, but over the years floods, rains, and wind have formed the curves in the rocks.

The reasons the inhabitants of the Canyon de Chelly National Monument in Arizona abandoned their elaborate cliffside villages around AD 1200 are unknown today. The federal government and the Navajo Nation jointly manage the preserve that protects the site.

At the center of Salt Lake City, Utah, the Salt Lake Temple and the Tabernacle sit in Temple Square. The temple took 40 years to build and was dedicated in 1893. The domed tabernacle is home to the famous Mormon Tabernacle Choir and an 11,623-pipe organ.

Utah's Arches National Park contains more than 2,000 natural sandstone arches. The park is a high desert area with extreme, fluctuating temperatures: summers are hot, winters are cold, and even in one day, temperatures can vary by as much as 50 degrees Fahrenheit (28 degrees Celsius).

All around the solitary hoodoo called Thor's Hammer, the Silent City of Utah's Bryce Canyon National Park rises from the canyon floor. Not a typical canyon, Bryce is shaped by freeze-thaw cycles, as opposed to by a river.

The oldest building in Idaho, the Mission of the Sacred Heart was constructed in the 1850s by the Jesuits and members of the Coeur d'Alene tribe. The interior was decorated in a colonial-chic style: painted newspapers on the walls, tin-can chandeliers, and wooden altars painted to resemble marble.

The Bear River flows through Cache Valley, agricultural land that extends over northern Utah and southern Idaho. The valley's name comes from the French *cacher*, which means "to hide," because mid-1800s trappers hid their furs in the area.

Route 66 was built in the 1920s to link Chicago and Los Angeles, but by the mid-1980s the Interstate Highway had made the road obsolete. Parts of the road, now called "Historic Route 66," still function, and are designated National Scenic Byways.

Dune evening primroses and desert sand verbena cover the sandy ground of Anza-Borrego Desert State Park, the largest state park in California. The park is named after the Spanish explorer Juan Bautista de Anza and the Spanish word *borrego,* which means "bighorn sheep."

Napa Valley is the most well-known and prestigious wine region in America. Today the area is home to more than 300 wineries, several of which date back to the 19th century.

Yosemite National Park in California contains many waterfalls that thunder in the spring but in other seasons trickle or stop altogether. Here, Bridalveil Fall tumbles into Yosemite Valley.

The Golden Gate Bridge was painted vermilion orange despite a request by the Navy to paint it black and yellow for visibility. However, the bridge is named not after its hue, but after the Golden Gate Strait, which connects San Francisco Bay to the Pacific Ocean.

The Santa Lucia Mountains rise out of the Pacific Ocean on the coastline of Big Sur in central California. In summer, drivers along the coastal Highway 1 experience the impression of flying, as foggy clouds cover the road and the cliffs beside the highway drop off into the ocean far below.

In 1771 the Carmel Mission Basilica was established by Father Junípero Serra, who led an expedition from New Spain (Mexico) to claim upper California. The mission closed in 1834 and the building deteriorated until restoration began in 1884. Now the mission is an active parish and school.

Since the early 1900s, Laguna Beach, California, has attracted painters and other artists, many of whom live here year round. Art fairs and festivals, as well as the community's seven sandy beaches, draw three million visitors a year.

The large winter waves off Oahu make the island a surfing haven. Polynesians brought the sport to Hawaii, and the chiefs used it to demonstrate their dominance over the commoners. In the 1800s missionaries discouraged and almost extinguished surfing, but it made a revival in the early 1900s.

The redwood trees in Redwood National Park grow to be some of the tallest in the world because of the cool climate and moist weather in northern California. The Pacific rhododendrons beneath the redwoods also grow tall because they must reach for the sun, which is largely hidden by the towering giants.

Lupines line the Oregon coast, and waves crash against the beach below. Temperatures in Oregon's Pacific waters range from a chilly 42 degrees Fahrenheit (6 degrees Celsius) in January to a refreshing 68 (20 degrees Celsius) in August.

Mount Hood looms above the Cascade mountain range, visible from these fields of blossoming pear trees and from the metropolitan area of Portland, Oregon.

Tlingit people were the first inhabitants of the area now known as Haines, Alaska, where visitors can still see historical Native American art, like totem poles, and purchase modern jewelry, carvings, and baskets. In the summer, a Chilkat theatre company performs contemporary versions of Native American myths at the Totem Village.

The Yentna Glacier in the Alaska Mountain range is classified as a surging glacier, meaning the glacial ice can move as fast as 4.2 feet (1.3 meters) per hour but can also be nearly stagnant for up to 50 years.